THE SECRET OF THE SEVEN SEALS

AF273148

Impressum
Original: THE BOOK OF LIGHT (Lanoo)
Library of Congress, Washington D.C.
TXU 451243, 02.01.1991
Copyright © Verlag Elke Straube
Schriftsatz und Gestaltung: Elke Straube
Covergestaltung: Verlag Elke Straube
Herstellung: Books on Demand GmbH
ISBN: 978-3-949377-10-5

THE SECRET OF THE SEVEN SEALS

LANOO
(Christian Anders)

In deep devotion to
Helena Petrovna Blavatsky
(1831-1891)
and to
Dr. Georg Grimm
(1868-1945)

TABLE OF CONTENTS

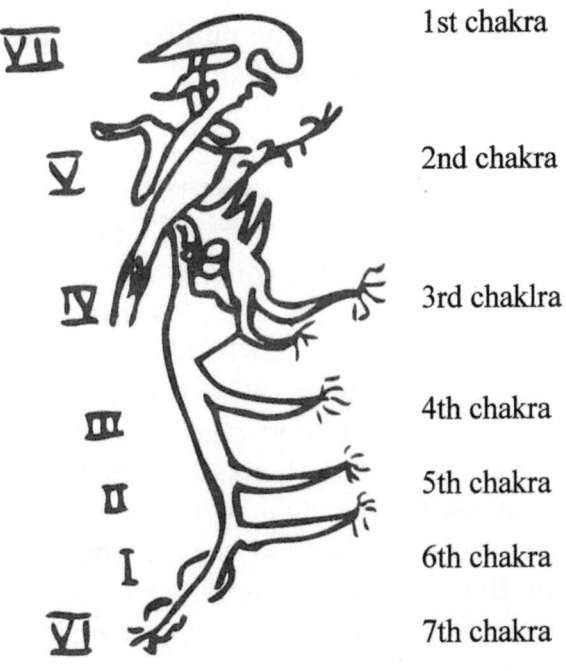

1st chakra

2nd chakra

3rd chaklra

4th chakra

5th chakra

6th chakra

7th chakra

The Seven Seals are the seven chakras of the human body, ruled by seven signs of the Zodiac constellation. The remaining five signs influence the etheric or prāṇa प्राण body. The seven cities, societies, trumpet calls and horsemen named in the bible (Apocalypse) are secret hints at the seven chakras, their corresponding organs and the sensations experienced by the candidate, for instance at

1

Initiation, when Kuṇḍalinī awakens and flows in the order of the numbering. Thus it is the 2nd chakra from below[1], which opens first and therefore becomes the first seal. Why? Because it is at the 2nd chakra from below where the positive and negative energy-currents start, together with two prāṇic nervestrings along the spine to meet again at the point between the eyes. See the esoteric description in "THE SERPENT", p. 11. It is also because the procreative organs are connected with the second chakra from below that Kuṇḍalinī starts here, since that chakra guarantees the survival of the species. Another reason for the 2nd chakra from below being the first seal is "the fall of man" about 18.000.000 B.C., but also the placing of the seals on man[2] prior to that. The opening of the seals or chakras and the resulting dramatic sensations in the candidate are described in symbolical form in the last book of the bible "Revelation", also known as "Apocalypse" and fully revealed in THE BOOK OF LIGHT. Once all seals or chakras are opened and conquered by the candidate through moral

---

1 Or the 6th from the top.
2 By angels.

purity and meditation, the candidate is dwīja द्विज or "Twiceborn" or "Born again" and has achieved immortality in consciousness. He can leave and re-enter his physical body at will. Thus death shall there be no more for him who overcame. AUM. He or she shall depart in full awareness from the body through the chakra on top of the head (7th seal) to then continue to live on the astral, mental and spiritual plane, teaching its denizens (deceased humans, angels, nature spirits etc.) that everything is TRANSIENT and that the purpose of life on ALL planes is NIRVĀṆA, the absence of desire.

The Seven Seals can also be awakened by Sound, for instance the Sound of the 49 letters (plus one) of the Sanskrit alphabet. The sound and beat of Rap, Rock, Punk, Disco etc. excites and awakes extremely and premature the lower seals or chakras, especially in younger people who have not yet conquered them and unleashes all the negative aspects (hate, anger, depression etc.) in their chakras, leading to the chaotic situation of today (crime, gangs, killing, moral and mental decay etc).

Before studying the seals and how to awaken them, the Lanoo should become acquainted with the Esoteric nature of the human spine, of whose anatomy orthodox science only knows little. I do, though, not concern myself here too much with what is already known about the human body. That can be looked up in any anatomy book[3]. I rather explain the etheric-astral-mental causes BEHIND the physical phenomena. Something about the esoteric anatomy of the human body has already been revealed in this book. Here now some additional information.

THE HUMAN BODY

The human body has four esoteric divisions:
1) Brain = organ of higher Mind
2) Lungs and heart = organs of lower Mind; lower but not necessarily negative
3) Navel = organ or rather centre of passional nature
4) Genitals = organs of reproduction[4]

THE NERVE SYSTEM

has dual aspects. 1) Cerebro-spinal = brain + spinal cord. 2) Sympathetic or ganglionic

---

3 Although even their physical definitions are often wrong.
4 When not used in sex-activity, they push Kuṇ-ḍalinī higher towards enlightenment.

system = series of distinct nerve-centres or ganglia[5] as seen in the illustration and later also in detail.

THE ASTRAL BODY

Man has 1 physical and 6 auric bodies, each existing on its own plane yet being united and carried by (and influencing) the physical body. Each physical organ has an astral counterpart. The astral body is made of 420,000 Nadis or channels, 3 major and a 4th running relative to the spinal column, this 4th beginning in the brain and ending at the tip or bottom end of the spine in a hollow channel (Kanda कन्द). 2 other major astral channels or astral nerves, Ida इद and Pinga-la पिन्गाल, begin at each nostril, run down along the spine, carrying etheric force, positive and negative, inhaled from the air. The etheric force manifests first at the 2nd chakra from below, where these two astral channels end or begin, however you want to see it. It is for that reason that the 2nd chakra[6] is the first seal.

---

5 Small masses of vascular neurine, extending at each side of the spine from head to coccyx.
6 From the bottom, but also 6th from top.

The inhalation process
works as follows: 1) Air passes into the nose.
2) A tiny valve at the nostril's root opens. 3)
Oxygen, nitrogen, hydrogen, krypton (watch
out Superman...) and other gases enter the
lungs. 4) Etheric energy or prāṇa runs along
the two astral nerves Ida and Pingala and
manifests in the 1st seal or 2nd chakra from
below, in our enumeration chakra number 6.
The nerve ganglia are listed as can be seen in
the illustration on the front page.

1) Conarium (Sahasrāva)
2) Cavernous (Ājnā)
3) Pharyngeal (Vishuddhi)
4) Cardiac (Anahata)
5) Epigastric (Manipuraka)
6) Prostatic (Adhisthana)
7) Sacral (sacred) ganglion (Muladhara),
Anal chakra. Abuse it and you pay the
price...

All the disastrous theories of Psychoanalysis
result from the fact that this "science" defines
man basically from his ANUS upwards, hen-
ce Anal[7]ysis. The reason: People like Freud
etc. were often themselves strongly under

---

7 Mod. Latin for anus = ANALIS...

the influence of their own anal or lower chakras. Once again it is the blind leading the blind, which in turn led to the billion Dollar business of today, called "Psychoanalysis".

THE PINEAL GLAND

is located in the brain behind the extremity of the third ventricle. Form: small conical, dark-grey body filled with phosphate and carbonate of lime. Once that material is touched by Kuṇḍalinī you will even shine visibly and experience enlightenment. This gland is the now atrophied first eye of the androgynous race. Below the pineal gland and behind the two eyes there is the pituitary gland, "seat of the soul". Both, pineal and pituitary, were once one.

THE BRAIN

The brain has 12 spiritual centres, influenced already at birth by the 12 signs of the Zodiac.

THE ENDOCRINE GLANDS

1) Pineal Gland, 2) Pituitary Gland, regulating growth, bone structure, associated also with genital organs, when touched by Kuṇḍalinī at orgasm, which leads to Kuṇḍalinī downwards, ripping a hole into the etheric chakra connecting you with the demon

world. A safer way would be to let K. accumulate naturally by abstaining from sexual activity. Then the orgasmic feeling is forever … and has not to be renewed by sexual activity. 3) The Thyroid Gland regulates production and distribution of thyroxin (complex iodine compound). Situated at the neck. Balances function of body, aids, digestion, elimination etc. 4) The Parathyroid Gland, placed in the Thyroid, regulates metabolism, calcium salts, lactic acid, phosphates. Important for the brain, nerve and sexfunction.

5) The Thymus Gland, situated at the chest. Large in children, small in adults. An important part of the immune system, controls heart function and glandular substances. We experience love there and only secondary in our heart. The reason why most people can't truly love somebody, even if they know they should, is because they are karmically born with a small Thymus Gland.

6) The Spleen, seat of the astral body. At death people often exude a smokelike substance from the spleen as witnessed by many M.D.s and nurses etc. Medical science thinks that the spleen, situated in the left upper quadrant of the abdomen, can destroy red blood cells and form antibodies against bac-

teria and other infections. This is nonsense. Read my book about AIDS[8], and you will understand. Fact is: Spleen and pituitary are connected, influencing the body as an operating triad. The spleen is also a filtration station within the body.

THE LUNGS

With each inhalation we receive from or rather through the lungs not only air, but also ātmic or prāṇic power from the astro-etheric plane, energizing also the astral and etheric body. We, like everything else, breathe because the universe expands and contracts or inhales and exhales.

THE HEART

is not a pump but a valve in the blood vascular system. It regulates the blood flow.

THE PROSTATE

is a gland near the backbone, where it contacts the lower part of the bladder. In man the Prostate is of the size of a baby's fist, in woman the Prostate is present too but much smaller. Most men have Prostatitis, a frequent complication of Gonorrhea. The ejacula-

---

8 "The Man W.H.O. Created AIDS".

ry tubes of the male testes enter the Prostate, between which and the pubis is the venous pudendal plexus, where the dorsal vein of the penis ends. The Prostate is THE FIRST SEAL. Those who conquer this seal shall conquer all the others, which is why I dedicate more time and space to the description of its function. The Prostate is the seat of the serpentine fire, the 6th chakra. When awakened, for instance through sexual activity, the Prostate excretes an oily substance. If we abstain from sexual activity, that oily substance enters the blood, where it is carried all over the body as part of the Serpentfire causing enlightenment in the brain.

The oily substance excreted by the Prostate and present in the blood of the celibate monk was called "CHRISM" by the Greeks. This "rising oil" or Chrism turned later into the rising Christ or "The blood of Christ" (Heb. 10:19; 1 Pet.1:2; 1In.1:7), or "the Christ in man". As the spleen is the seat of the Astral body, the Prostate is the centre of it, from which rise 72,000 Nadis, composed of astral matter carrying psychic currents. The 2 most important of these Nadis are Ida and Pingala. THEY are in truth "the thieves" crucified at each side of Jesus who is here but a symbol for the Sushumna, the hollow channel at the tip of the spine. That too is like "a cup" which, when filled with "Chrism" or seminal fluid, that fluid, when rising in the chaste candidate, becomes "The rising Christ".

"THE SERPENT"

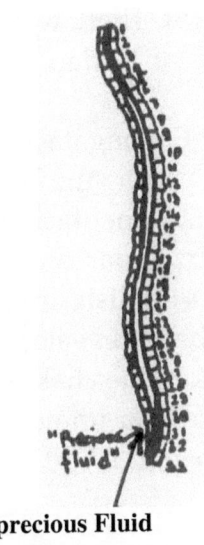

precious Fluid

... is the human spine or Columna Spinalis with 33 segments of bone, resembling a serpent standing perpendicular on its tail. Once Kuṇḍalinī has crossed all 33 segments up to the highest, the candidate became enlightened, which is why "Jesus lived for 33 years." Or: Jesus was ENLIGHTENED.

The centre canal of the bony column is filled with the "precious fluid of enlightenment", made of the body's air gases (expl. only orally). It is that spinal fluid, when activated by and mixed with Kuṇḍalinī, which becomes "the River of God" by which, for instance, Jesus like every other Initiate was "baptized" in Jordan (Mat.2:13,15). There was in those days never a real river of Jordan, known by that name.

It is the Medulla Oblongata which connects the Spinal cord with the brain, causing symptoms like migraine, headaches etc., being nothing but irregular outbreaks of Kuṇḍalinī caused by a foolish, immoral lifestyle etc. Enough has been revealed to enable the candidate to awaken the chakras or seals and thus return to his or her immortal, uncreated, eternal, timeless being. AUM.

THE AWAKENING OF THE SEALS

The Seals must be awakened in the order 1, 2, 3, 4, 5, 6, 7 or when counted as chakras 6, 5, 4, 3, 2, 7 and 1 (top chakra). The Seals are awakened by study, meditation and no sexual activity and by SOUND, the sound of the corresponding Sanskrit letters who were spoken millions of years ago by Deva Angels when they placed the seals on a - in the beginning still sexless - human race. AUM. The corresponding Sanskrit letters are the keys opening the seal. In order to use or pronounce these letters properly one has to study the Sanskrit alphabet.

MAN WITH SEVEN CHAKRAS
(and the connected organs and chakras)

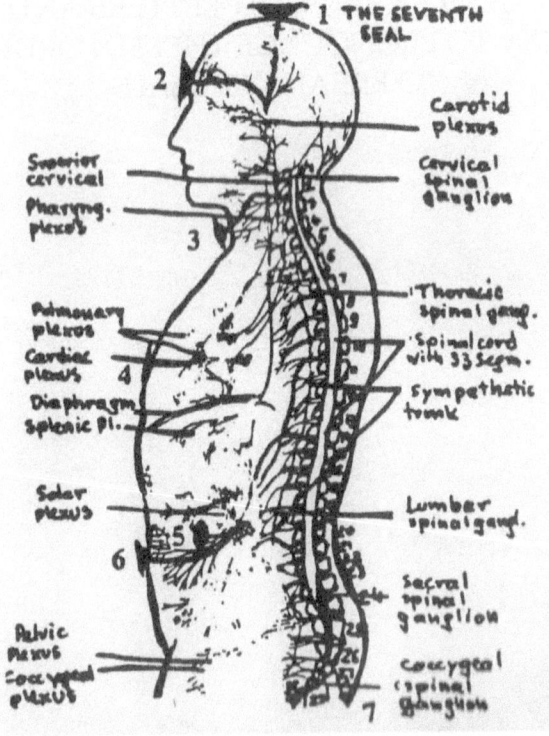

THE 49 + 1 SANSKRIT LETTERS AND HOW TO PRONOUNCE THEM IN ORDER TO BREAK THE SEALS

अ (a), आ (ā), इ (i), ई (ī),
उ (u), ऊ (ū), ऋ (ṛi), ॠ
(ṛī), ऌ (ḷri), ॡ (ḷrī),
ए (e), ऐ (ai), ओ (o), औ (au),
ं (aṃ, m or ṇ), ः (aha, ḥ),
क (ka), ख (kha), ग (ga), घ
(gha), ङ (ṅa), च (cha), छ
(chha), ज (ja), झ (jha)
ञ (ña), ट (ṭa), ठ (ṭha),
ड (ḍa), ढ (ḍha), ण (ṇa),
त (ta), थ (tha), द (da), ध
(dha), न (na), प (pa), फ (pha),
ब (ba), भ (bha), म (ma),
य (ya), र (ra), ल (la), व (va),
श (śa), ष (sha), स (sa), ह
(ha), [क्ष (ksha)].

Why 49 + 1 letters?

There are 49 letters but if we add the conso-
nant "ksha" we receive 50 letters, which,
when 20 times uttered, open the 1000 pe-
talled chakra on top of your head, the seventh seal.

अ = a, like the a in org_an or the u in b_ut.

आ = ā, like the a in c_ar but twice as long.

इ = i, like the i in p_in.

ई = ī, like the e in m_e but twice as long.

उ = u, like the u in p_ush

ऊ = ū, like the u in r_ule but held twice as long.

ऋ = ri, like the ri in R_ita but more like the French r_u.

ॠ = rī, same as ri but the i held twice as long.

ऌ = lri, like lri (the ri from R_ita).

ॡ = lrī, like lri but the i held twice as long.

ए = e, like the e in th<u>e</u>y.

ऐ = ai, like the ai in <u>ai</u>sle.

आे = o, like the o in g<u>o</u>.

आै = au, like the ow in h<u>ow</u>

ं = aṃ, moṛ n, like the nasal n in the French word bo<u>n</u>.

: aha, ḥ, pronounced as written with the a's like in org<u>an</u>.

क = ka, like the k in <u>k</u>ite and the a in org<u>an</u>.

रव = kha, like the kh in Ec<u>kh</u>art and the a in org<u>an</u>.

ग=ga, like the g in give and the a in organ.

घ=gha, like the gh in dig-hard and the a in organ.

ङ=ṅa, like the n in sing and the a in organ.

च=cha, like the ch in chair and the a in organ.

छ=chha, like the chh in staunch-heart.

ज=ja, like the j in joy and the a in organ.

झ=jha, like the dgeh in

hedgehog and the a in
organ.
ञ = ña, like the ñ in cañyon
and the a in organ.
ट = ṭa, like the t in ṭub
and a in organ.
ठ = ṭha, like the t h in
light-heart and a in organ.
ड = ḍa, like the d in ḍove and
the a in organ.
ढ = ḍha, like the dh in reḍhot
and the a in organ.
ण = ṇa, like in rṇa but pre-
pare to say ṇa, + a in organ.

त=ta, like the t in ten, and the a in organ.

थ=tha, like the t h in fight her and a like in organ.

द=da, like the the d in dance and a in organ.

ध=dha, like the d h in sold house and the a in organ.

न=na, like the n in name and the a in organ.

प=pa, like punk and organ.

फ=pha, like the p h in

help <u>h</u>im, plus the a in or-
g<u>a</u>n.
ब = ba, like the b in <u>b</u>omb,
and the a in org<u>a</u>n.
भ = bha, like the b h in
bom<u>b</u> <u>h</u>ere, and the a
in org<u>a</u>n.
म = ma, like the m in
<u>m</u>other, plus the a in or-
g<u>a</u>n.
य = ya, like the y in <u>y</u>ou
plus the a in org<u>a</u>n.
र = ra, like ital. <u>R</u>oma
plus the a in org<u>a</u>n.

ल = la, like the l in <u>l</u>ove and the a in org<u>a</u>n.

व = va or wa, like the v in <u>v</u>el<u>v</u>et and the a in org<u>a</u>n.

शा = śa, like the sh in <u>sh</u>oe, but more spoken with the back of the mouth-roof, and a as in org<u>a</u>n.

ष = sha, like the sh in <u>sh</u>ine and the a in org<u>a</u>n.

स = sa, like the s in <u>s</u>and, and the a in org<u>a</u>n.

ह =ha, like the h in <u>hun</u>-
ter and the a in org<u>a</u>n.

क्ष =ksha, like the ksh
in r<u>iksh</u>a and the a in or-
g<u>a</u>n. The Sanskrit letters
are very powerful. Just look-
ing at them for 15 minutes
and longer activates the
chakras.

(Handwritten by Lanoo)

On the next pages you shall find the 50
Sanskrit letters or "Seal openers" in different
occult formations.
Look at them and experience …

THE POWER
OF
THE SEVEN SEALS

25

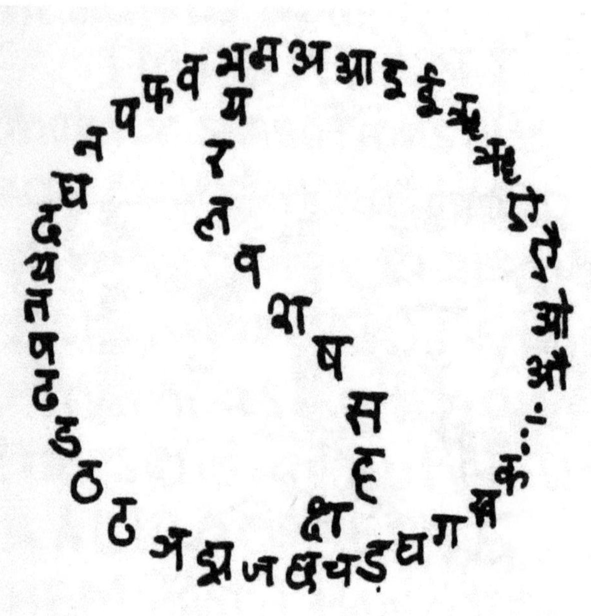

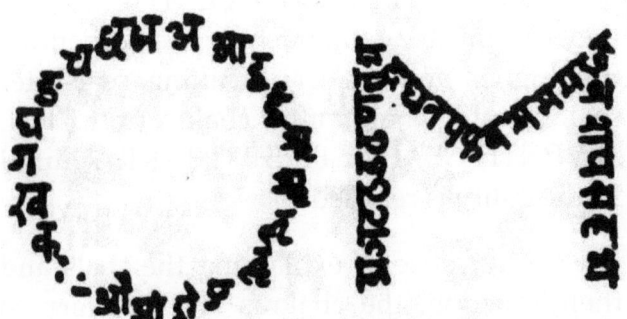

27

WRITING the letters (see THE BOOK OF LIGHT) opens the seals as well.

IMPORTANT

Whatever sensations one may experience at the opening of the seals, he or she must NOT yield to them (as Koresh and others did...) but NEUTRALLY OBSERVE THEM until they disappear again, pushing the Serpentine fire higher and higher, breaking seal after seal, opening chakra after chakra up to THE SEVENTH SEAL or FIRST CHAKRA[9], until Immortality is reached.

For the purpose of explaining the seals and their function, the chakras are, contrary to other systems, enumerated from the top (1st chakra) to the bottom (7th chakra), since enlightenment occurs in the top chakra, which makes it the highest and therefore number one, although the (eventually liberating) Kuṇḍalinī force is awakened in the bottom chakras first.

AUM

---

9 From the top.

THE FIRST SEAL I
The Sixth Chakra (from the top)

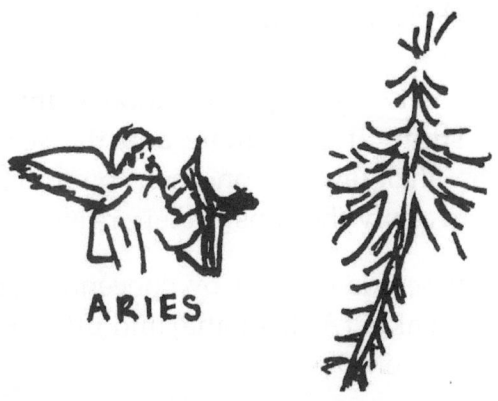

ARIES

Prostatic ganglion. Sensations at the awakening: Phallic, sexcenter, symbolized in the bible as "the city of Smyrna", noted for fig industry.

"When the lamb opened one of the Seals ... behold a white horse ... who was riding him had a bow." Rev. 6,12. "One of the seals" is another veil to hide the Truth before the masses, in order to keep them in bondage where they are the weakest - in their sexdrive. "The white horse" indicates that it is here, where purity has to be achieved, namely by overcoming the sexdrive, abstain from procreative activity and thus allow "the Christ to rise" - meaning Kuṇḍalinī. "The Bowman" is you, the conqueror. Before I reveal to you the letters, opening the first seal, let me emphasize that THE SAFEST WAY to open the seals is a pure lifestyle (no sex, no drugs, no alcohol), eat only vegetarian food, drink only water, study and meditate and the seals or chakras shall awake on their own. THEN you may apply the Sanskrit letters etc.

The first seal is opened by concentration on the 6th Chakra (Adhisthana) and uttering the Sanskrit letters 39-44:

ब भ म य र ल or ba (39), bha (40), ma (41), ya (42), ra (43), la (44)

Pronounce the a like the u in "but". After having pronounced the letters, you concentrate on the next seal or chakra and speak or just think the corresponding letters. Writing has the same effect, but without STUDYING the Sanskrit alphabet as taught in THE BOOK OF LIGHT shall be no result at all. "The trumpet call" at the opening of the first seal announces "hail and fire, mixed with blood … cast into the earth … ⅓ of the earth was consumed, ⅓ of the trees and all fresh grass were consumed." (ch. 8:7). That points at the awakening of the psychic consciousness being ⅓ of our nature. "Hail" is the lunar element in us, being violently experienced. "Fire" is the solar force, waiting from above to be mixed with the blood and/or Earth - Kuṇḍalinī, shooting upwards through our feet, meeting "at the marriage of the lamb" the Sun-Kuṇḍalinī at the opening of the 7th Seal.

The "ONE THIRD" alludes also to "The fall of Man" or to the refusal of " … ⅓ of the angels to give mind to an until then mindless race, which led to the war in heaven" (see BOOK OF LIGHT). The first seal is under the influence of ARIES, "the Bowman".

THE SECOND SEAL II
The Fifth Chakra (from the top)

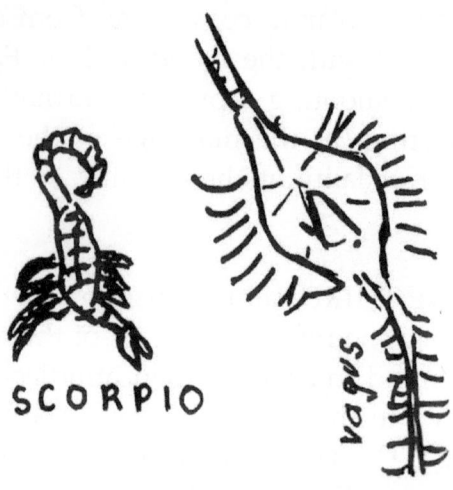

SCORPIO

vagus

Epigastric ganglion. Sensation at the awakening: Psychic forces, symbolized in the bible as "the city of Pergamos", noted for psychic temples. "When he opened the second seal... a fiery red horse came out... who was riding him... was given a great sword." (Rev.6:3,4). The red horse points at the abdominal region, its "rider" passion personified (also the red Dragon etc.). Opening that seal prematurely unleashes passion.

The second seal is opened by concentrating on it and uttering the Sanskrit letters 29-38 or

उ ढ ण त थ द ध न प
फ

or ḍa (29), ḍha (30), ṇa (31), ta (32), tha
(33), da (34), dha (35), na (36), pa (37),
pha (38).

The trumpet call at the opening of the second
seal announced a "great flaming mountain of
fire" as if he "was cast into the sea". And
again "⅓ of the sea came to blood. The third
of the existent beings in the sea, having
souls, died and the ⅓ of the ships[10] were
wrecked" (ch.8:8,9).

The flaming mountain is (also) the symbol of
Mars, ruling our lower nature, "the sea". Only the one who has mastered passion and
carnal desire shall survive the opening of the
seal.

David Koresh, Swaggart and others didn't or
will not survive. The 2nd seal is ruled by
Scorpio (Mars house, War God).

---

10 Also ⅓ of the planets of the Makara.

THE THIRD SEAL III
The fourth Chakra (from the top)

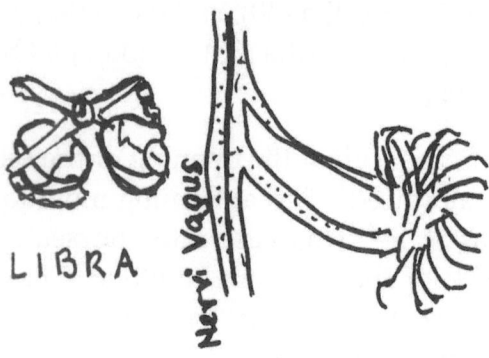

LIBRA

Nervi Vagus

Cardiac ganglion. Sensations at the awakening: Joy and depression, symbolized as the city of Thyateira since it manufactures scarlet (refers to circulatory system). "When he opened the 3rd seal... a black horse. Who was riding him had a balance in his hand" (ch.6: 5,6). Black horse = lower mind. Balance = This seal is under Libra. 3rd seal is anahata or heart chakra. In the heart a distinction is drawn between spiritual and non-spiritual mind (intellect, tainted by psychic emotions and carnal desires). Make no mistake, the greatest cultures, for instance ours, were created by that non-spiritual mind, which tells you something about the "greatness" of these cultures. The 3rd seal is opened by the Sanskrit letters 17-28:

क ख ग घ ङ च छ ज
झ ञ ट ठ

or ka (17), kha (18), ga (19), gha (20),
ṅa (21), cha (22), chha (23), ja (24),
jha (25), ña (26), ṭa (27), ṭha (28)

Don't even try to pronounce them without having studied the alphabet as taught in THE BOOK OF LIGHT and in this book, it won't work. Your chakras will not react.

At the 3rd trumpet call "a star flaming like a storch" fell from the sky on "the third of the rivers and on the springs of waters". "Worm-wood" was the name of the star, tainting the water, killing many men because "they (the waters) were made bitter" (ch.8:10,11). Venus is the falling star, affecting the emotional psychic nature. "The bitter waters" symboli-ze: All pleasure eventually produces pain. But once man's nature is purified and has at-tained absence of desire, leading to Nirvāṇa, his "bitter waters" also the body's vital essen-ce, transmute through a celibate life of study and meditation into 'the sweet waters of life'.

THE FOURTH SEAL IV
The Third Chakra

VIRGO

Laryngeal ganglion. Sensations at the opening: "Tasting the word". We can literally taste Kuṇḍalinī, since it touches the Adam's apple. Therefore the symbol is the "city of Sardeis", pointing at a sardion, sardine or carnelian. "When he opened the Fourth seal…: Come… a dun horse… riding him… was death and the unseen went along with him" (ch.6:7,8).

"The dun horse" is the lowest sex division, THE driving power in or of everybody's lower self. There is no true liberation from anything until somebody has not conquered or rather detached oneself from that power (over him…). Sex exists in two realms, psychic and physical, during life AND after death on the lower astral planes (even right now during life of the physical body). All desires can only be conquered not by yielding to them but rather by attaining more and more neutrality, until they fall off from you. During the process of detachment and thus overcoming, your desires may grow stronger and threaten to overwhelm you, by turning into "the Beast" and thus the true enemy which is you, or rather what you are NOT.

Remain strong, remain neutrally OBSERVENT, WITNESSING everything. While the rest of the world yield to their desires, thus becoming more and more enslaved to them, you attack and destroy them single handed, just by observing and NOT yielding to them.

Beware of THE BEAST! It is nowhere out there, not even some New World ORDER computer-controlled Supersatellite, the Beast is in and around YOU, it is what you are NOT, and you are not your body, emotion, mind, soul and even spirit. AUM.

THE BEAST in and around you
(Ill. Ron Lennstrom)

The Fourth seal is opened by concentrating on the 5th chakra (vishuddhi) and uttering the Sanskrit letters 1-16:

अ आ इ ई उ ऊ ऋ ॠ ऌ ॡ ए ऐ
ओ औ ं ः

or a (1), ā (2), i (3), ī (4), u (5), ū (6), ṛi (7), ṛī (8), lṛi (9), lṛī (10), e (11), ai (12), o (13), au (14), ṃ (15), ḥ (16)

The 4th trumpet call given by the 4th divinity caused that "⅓ of the sun was stricken" as well as ⅓ of moon and stars, "and the day should not give light to it" and likewise the night. It means that only when the physical and psychic forces have been brought into equilibrium and neutralized each other, consciousness can rise to a higher plane. Or: Only when you have detached yourself from the lower you can rise to the higher. The ruling Zodiac of the 4th seal, 3rd chakra is virgo. Only if you become a virgo or virgin again you can master

THE FIFTH SEAL V
The second Chakra (from the trop)

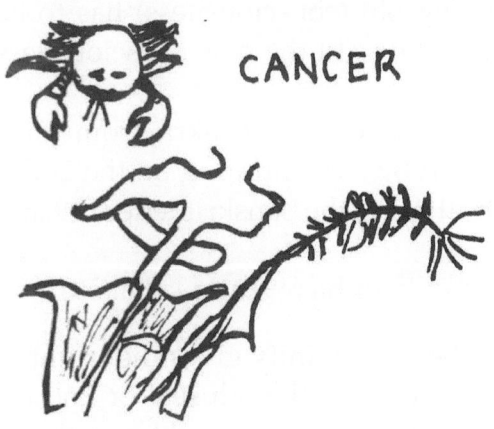

CANCER

Cavernous ganglion. Sensation at the awakening: Earthquake like, violently overwhelming but eventually leading to enlightenment. Symbol: City of Philadelphia because repeatedly destroyed by earthquakes. In ch. 6:9-11 we read: "When he opened the fifth seal, I saw... those... sacrified... until their fellow slaves and... brothers... should have finished."

Only a small percentage of our brain (cells) is actually functioning. The rest, when touched by Kuṇḍalinī, is enlightened and "sacrificed". But first the other centres or "their brothers" have to be activated by study and meditation or "killed" as the bible has it. Why killed? Because the term "killed" often indicates that something old (consciousness) has to be killed or to die until the new consciousness can arise.

The 5th seal or 2nd chakra from above is awakened by concentrating on the 2nd chakra and uttering the Sanskrit letters 49 and 50:

ह क्ष or ha (49) and ksha (59)

When the 5th Divinity gives the trumpet call at the opening of the 5th seal or 2nd chakra "a star had fallen from the sky to the earth" and "sun and air were darkened by smoke "and" … came locusts upon the earth". Like "scorpions on the earth have license". The meaning is clear: The fallen star is Venus, in its lower aspect, exiting passions and desires in man and woman, clouding them in smoke. The scorpion-like cavalry are impure thoughts. These "scorpions have license" to "punish men five months". the 5 months of the summertime are meant, when passions and desires are most active (see ch.9:1-12). Cancer rules the Fifth Seal.

THE SIXTH SEAL VI
The Seventh Chakra (from the top)
At the bottom of the spine

Sacral ganglion, Muladhara Chakra. Sensations, when awakened: Regenerative Forces, but also anger, hatred and selfishness, all manifesting and hiding there in the anal area. Life is an ocean of suffering, the forbidden fruit, a place totally inappropriate for us. We, like everything else, belong where we came from, we belong to, we ARE at our core,

NIRVĀṆA

A search for Truth in any other direction will lead eventually to moral and physical decay. Primitive beats and rhythms (Rap, Rock, Disco, Hip Hop etc.) are enjoyed by those whose anal chakras are being opened by low consciousness. The result: A society ruled by crime and perversion from the top to the bottom. The fish rots and stinks always from the head (government) first. Symbol for the 2nd chakra: The Diana Temple in Ephesos. Perverted rites were running wild there. Or: An awakening of the Kuṇḍalinī before moral purity is attained causes perversion and death. Therefore we read in ch.6:12-17: "...when he opened the sixth seal... came a great earthquake". Here the earthquake means a trauma in the brain (5th seal), either enlightening or destroying the candidate. Why even the candidate, who has already achieved moral purity? Because Kuṇḍalinī, once reaching the (almost) highest or 2nd chakra from the top, rushes then down to the lowest and 7th chakra. The slightest hidden impurity would cause Kuṇḍalinī or the Serpentfire to rush further downwards and often kill the candidate. IF Kuṇḍalinī can be reversed there by the champion, it shall then rush back and upwards and hit the candidate once again in the brain. You see now why any other test or problem or also achievement in life is a child's play, compared to "the trials, tribulations and ordeals of Initiation"?

The 6th seal is opened by the letters 45-48

व श ष स
or wa(45), śa (46), sha (47), sa (48)

The sixth Trumpet call "turns loose the four Divinities who are fettered at the great river Euphrates" and "they should kill the third of men". The river Euphrates is the cerebro-spinal axis, and the 4 divinities rule the seasons, but also symbolize the religious worship mentality of those ⅓ who indulge, for instance in the insanity of religion of today. The 6th Seal (7th chakra from the top) is ruled by Capricorn. How to rule and dominate a person? In every person, no matter how powerful or intelligent, there is a child or THE child hidden. Once you "discover" that child you speak to it and thus you influence but also change that person easily to the better (see the SEVEN RAYS, Book of Light). Once the 6th seal is opened the candidate experiences sheer terror. He becomes aware of the EMPTINESS in everything, since we are basically made of gaps, being between the atoms and molecules of our bodies and also around and between us. The Buddha reveals: "As I tarried there (meditating alone in the forest) a deer came by, a bird caused a twig to fall, and the wind set all the leaves whispering; and I thought: 'Now it is coming - that fear and terror'." The 6th Seal is ruled by

THE SEVENTH SEAL VII
(The First Chakra - top of the head)

Pineal gland. Sensation: ENLIGHTEN-
MENT. Symbol: City of Laodikeia, noted for
the manifacture of "Phrygian powder or eye-
salve", pointing at the 3rd eye and higher.

"When he opened the 7th seal... silence...
(then) 7 trumpets." When Kuṇḍalinī flows
through the seven and twelve braincentres a
sound is heard (Rev. 8:1-6). "He is born" - "It
is done." Meaning that the candidate has suc-
cessfully passed the test of Initiation while
having been <u>bound</u> at a cross and not nailed,
as religion wants us to believe (see THE
BOOK OF LIGHT). The first seal is opened
by uttering the Sanskrit letters 1-50. The
trumpet call at the opening, given by the 7th
Divinity in ch.11:15-18 causes "great voices in
the sky" and " ... his Anointed shall reign
throughout the aeons and aeons."

The opening of the highest chakra causes
immortality in consciousness and we hear
the voices of the highest angels, telling us
that we shall rule and live throughout "the
aeons of the aeons", which would be at most
311,040,000,000,000 years, but THEN everything including the highest heavens shall be
destroyed to reawake again after Māha-Pra-
laya of 311,040,000,000,000 years, which is
why the Buddha who had attained enlight-

enment with all seals or chakras opened, uttered as answer to the angelic revelation (as written in ch11:15-18): "And if I would only be reborn among the highest Gods, I do not want to return to this world. I have nothing anymore in common with the order of the things." So he chose NIRVĀṆA, which is higher than the highest heavens with all their Gods and God itself.

Thus Gautama Buddha can truly be called "the teacher of men AND Gods". AUM.

The Seventh Seal and First Chakra is ruled by LEO. The cycle is closed. Kuṇḍalinī, the Serpent, swallows its own tail by rushing from the lowest Chakra or 6th Seal, ruled by CAPRICORN to the highest 1st chakra or Seventh Seal, ruled by LEO.

The opening of The Seventh Seal leads to ...

ENLIGHTENMENT

Jesus at the moment of enlightenment, after having been initiated by his Guru, the "Melchizedek" of the bible.

ESOTERIC VOCABULARY

<u>Chakra</u> चक्र, Sanskrit "wheel". Etheric energy-vortex, connected with the prāṇic circulations and ganglia of the Auric Egg (human aura), thus functioning in the physical body through the intermediary of the linga-śarīra रव लिन्ग शरीर (astral body). The location and function of the Chakras is described in this book and in THE BOOK OF LIGHT.

Kuṇḍalinī कुण्डलिनी, Sanskrit "circular", "winding", "spiral", "coiling" action or energy becomes Kuṇḍalinī in man. Kuṇḍalinī works in or on man through his auric egg. K. is situated at the base of the spine. Kuṇḍalinī is directed by thought. Beware of Kuṇḍalinī! If directed downwards it shall destroy you. Detachment from body, emotion, mind soul and spirit causes Kuṇḍalinī to rise, leading to liberation from the wheel of life and death.

Nirvāṇa निर्वाण, Sanskrit "nir" (<u>out</u>), "vāṇa" from "vā" (to blow). Nirvāṇa is "out blown" or "annihilated". But only the lower principles in man are outblown or annihilated. Nirvāṇa is higher than (and very different from) any heaven, even higher than the union with or in Brahman.

Nirvāṇa is the absence of desire
and the ultimate destination
of all life forms.
We come from Nirvāṇa,
we go to Nirvāṇa.

AUM

The author

LANOO (Christian Anders) and the BOOK OF LIGHT

311,040,000,000,000 years of human and cosmic evolution. Where we come from, where we are, where we go to.

THE BOOK OF LIGHT will be the guiding scripture for the entire universe with everything in it. It unites all religions, philosophies, political systems and sciences in the world. You can choose between NIRVĀṆA and reincarnation.

May all beings attain the end of suffering. OM.

More books by LANOO (Christian Anders) in English

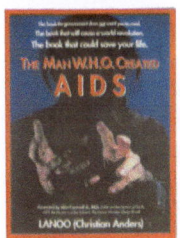
The Man W.H.O. created AIDS
ISBN: 978-3-3831106226; 514
pages

Two in one book! Englisch and
German!
Die Botschaft des wahren Gottes
NIRVĀNA &
Divine Message from the True
God;
ISBN: 978-3-937699-13-4;
268 pages

The Book of Light for children
ISBN: 978-3-937699-81-3;
46 pages

Order here:

Verlag Elke Straube
01778 Geising,
Lindenallee 18
Fon: 0174/13 34 337
Fax: 035056/23784
www.straube-verlag.com
e-mail: elke.straube@web.de

or
www.amazon.de
bookshop@bod.de